Trespassing

Poems from Ireland

George MacBeth

Hutchinson

London Sydney Auckland Johannesburg

This edition first published in 1991 by Hutchinson

Random Century Group Ltd
20 Vauxhall Bridge Road, London SW1V 2SA

Random Century Australia (Pty) Ltd
20 Alfred Street, Milsons Point, Sydney, NSW 2061, Australia

Random Century New Zealand Ltd
PO Box 40–086, Glenfield, Auckland 10, New Zealand

Random Century South Africa (Pty) Ltd
PO Box 337, Bergvlei, 2012, South Africa

British Library Cataloguing in Publication Data

MacBeth, George *1932–*
   Trespassing: poems from Ireland.
   I. Title
   821.914
ISBN 0-09-174825-9

Set in Ehrhardt by 🅰 Tek Art Ltd, Addiscombe, Croydon, Surrey
Printed and bound by Cox & Wyman Ltd, Reading

ng

ıS

Poetry

The Broken Places
A Doomsday Book
The Colour of Blood
The Night of Stones
A War Quartet
The Burning Cone
Collected Poems, 1958–1970
The Orlando Poems
Shrapnel
A Poet's Year
Lusus
In the Hours Waiting for the
   Blood to Come
Buying a Heart
Poems of Love and Death
Poems from Oby
The Long Darkness
The Cleaver Garden
Anatomy of a Divorce
Collected Poems, 1958–1982

Autobiography

My Scotland
A Child of the War

Children's Books

Noah's Journey
Jonah and the Lord
The Rectory Mice
The Book of Daniel

Novels

The Transformation
The Samurai
The Survivor
The Seven Witches
The Born Losers
A Kind of Treason
Anna's Book
The Lion of Pescara
Dizzy's Woman

Anthologies

The Penguin Book of Sick
Verse
The Penguin Book of Animal
Verse
Poetry 1900–1975
The Penguin Book of
Victorian Verse
The Falling Splendour
The Book of Cats
Poetry For Today

Contents

FOREWORD

The act of trespassing is a more or less venial sin,
depending on one's view of the rights of ownership. I
suspect that the peace of mind of a reader – on which all
poets trespass – is no more vulnerable than the paths
through woods and fields. If poems commit an act of
absolute trespass, then perhaps they do so only by virtue of
their claims on language. The sense of living in a country
where language matters comes quickly to the new Irish
resident, and he will frequently be reminded that he is
amongst – as Oscar Wilde remarked – 'the best talkers
since the Greeks'. These poems are a response to the
people of Ireland and the life their author has been
leading in County Galway since he settled there in 1988. I
hope they contain an undercurrent of willingness to wrestle
with the complex and bitter legacy of the planters, the
English and Scottish land-owners who have trespassed in
Ireland down the years. But more than this, in their
preoccupation with character and narrative, I hope they
express an admiration for the rich variety of human nature
in Ireland, and with its unbroken delight in the sinuosities
of the tongue, the trespasses of the art of blarney.

Trespassing

Wearing thick spectacles, a plump shape in a plum coat,
I see her at a distance, wavering slightly
As her bicycle negotiates the pot-holes.

She dismounts by the gate, where we stand talking.
Welcome to Moyne, she says gravely.
Do you like it here? It's nice, isn't it?

Indicating the weather, the façade, the cows,
The line of grey buildings to her right, the lime trees.

A woman of about forty, maybe living on a farm
Surrounded by goats and geese, sheep and horses,
She points to her Hercules brake. It's sticking, she says.

The old bike sticking. But it still keeps going.
Then she looks at me quizzically, with a smile.
The doctor said you'd be too proud to speak
To your neighbours. He was wrong there, anyway.

Then she's off, a smile, and a glint of eyes
Behind marred glass, a woman separated, I know,
From her husband, living alone, eager for acquaintance

On a neighbour's land, even a strange pair like us,
Foreigners from England, kin of the enemy.

But here I think, as I go indoors laughing,
There are no enemies, not even the hovering crows
Trespassing like her, acceptably, sociable chatterers.

Five Roads

Five roads lead out of Tuam.

One goes down past the paint-shop
To the river and the mill.

One goes close to the Post Office
And the launderette
And then reaches the old railway station.

One passes the doctor's
And the new car-park
On its way to the Roman Catholic Cathedral.

One leads by the seven schools
And the three solicitors
And then lands you at the Hermitage Hotel.

And one goes to the Travel Agent
And the Cake Box
On its way to the Protestant Cathedral of St Mary.

These are the five roads
In and out of Tuam
And all come back to The Square
Where the Cross rises behind its railings.

Remembering the Bad Things

For instance, every time he drove down that road
In the dark, or even during the day, in sunlight,
He remembered the small grey streak from the hedgerow

And then the slight impact, nothing very significant
In a big car, and wondering for several seconds
What it was he had struck, maybe the sheepdog

That was always rushing out under his wheels,
Crouching and then attacking, as if he was a stranger
And not the familiar large shape that rolled by every day.

But no, it was no dog. He remembered stopping
The car a hundred yards on, and reversing back
To where the once-living rag lay in the road.

He remembered opening the door, and walking forward
In the blaze of his headlamps, full beam in the dark
On the sprawl of a long cat, a toothpaste of blood

Oozing out of its mouth, and the eyes wide
On the far side of the road it would never reach.
Oh yes, he remembered the tears coming, useless tears

For not being careful enough, and then he remembered
Lifting the little corpse in his arms, warm and limp,
And laying it aside to rest for ever in the grass.

There were other bad things, but this was the one
He always remembered, knowing his own three cats
Alive and safe in the house, not half a mile away,

And someone crying, like him, for the loss of a dear one.

Itinerants

Seeing their donkey cropping grass
Outside my library, I remember the cart
It was drawing, loaded with branches,
And the two boys
Polite, and innocent, as I reprimanded them.

It's my wood. Is it, though? What is 'mine'
Or 'theirs' to the travelling people, lightless
In shacks beside an affluence of timber
Growing free
In a wood established from before Cromwell?

I walk through lopped limbs
Of sycamores, disturbing the cuttings
Abandoned on tarmac, distracting my car
When it rolls by
With the tyres crackling on scattered twigs.

The donkey flexes its ears. It brays
All night sometimes, and assembles dung
Purple as hippopotamuses, and steamy
Like vegetables,
On the concrete floor of what seemed my garage.

A fine day, one boy says, dismounting
From a bicycle, and I agree with him
Yielding a right of way, like wood,
To good manners,
And a sense of the common ownership of Ireland.

More theirs than mine. Here as a foreigner
I think of money supplying power
And how power begets nothing beyond vanity
And the priest's hole
Winding away from Moyne Park through the penal times.

Much is to be forgiven. Give a little
And take a little, a pile of donkey-shit
That looks pretty and feeds flower-beds
In exchange for a cart of logs
To keep a family warm. It's a fair bargain.

The Parable of the Shepherd

So imagine the man, lying awake in the dark
Beside his wife, after he knew that the strayed sheep
Was in his field, seeing it white in the rain, hearing it
                                                    calling.

Imagine him rising and dressing, saying to his wife
I'd better go and see what's wrong, it may be caught
On the wire, I could free it perhaps before the shepherd
                                                    comes.

Imagine him putting on his greatcoat, and crossing the
                                                    drive,
And opening the wicket gate, following the call
Of the sheep, and then hearing the call of its lamb

Separated on the other side of a barbed wire fence.
Imagine the man trying to steer the sheep
To where the big lamb was calling for its milk

On the other side of his wall. Imagine the dyke
Sheer, and the sheep knowing it couldn't jump
Without breaking a leg, and leaving its lamb starving.

And then imagine the man giving up, returning to bed
Out of the cold, out of the squelching bog of his field,
Leaving the sheep and the lamb to their own sad fortune.

And imagine him sleepless there, not making love
To his wife, hearing those bleating calls all night
In his brain, awake and in dreams, the calls of the lost

Whom no one, not even Jesus Christ in his glory,
Can restore to their own kind, to each other's love.

A Silver Gondola

Perhaps it happened. Or perhaps it didn't. I don't know.
But the detail about the silver gondola
Sticks in my mind, or should I say, my craw.

Picture the level water, twilight, a kind of Wagnerian
Funeral sort of craft
With a gaunt, moustachioed volunteer plying his oar

For a reasonable pittance. The bride
In a black Florentine brocaded night-gown
And a tricorne hat, the groom

Very elegant in his cape, with a cane
Long enough to probe the deepest mud in the channels.
                                                    And who
Are these? Who is anyone

Wanting a new start with a flirt of style
In another country, over a waste of canals,
Dark as the ditches littering the past in Norfolk.

Someone told me the story. Someone said
They got married, the ghost of happiness
And the friend of perfection. Good luck to them.

I say good luck to them, and I mean
To mean it. Except that sometimes
That fish-bone of the silver gondola still tickles my throat.

Bull Among the Daffodils

Once upon a time, in County Roscommon,
I was driving along when I came on a bull
In a field of daffodils. The bull had his head down
And his pizzle hanging, and he was an old bull
With his muddy tail swinging to keep the flies off.

He looked like a bull waiting for the estocada.

But he had some fight left. As I found out
When I climbed the wall, and went for a flower or two.
He came at me with his sawn-off horns up
And his tail going
In a last-ditch break for pardon.

I turned and ran, jumping the wall
To safety, and watching him breathing death at me, from
                                        the other side.

Of course, he didn't. I made this all up
Wanting to seem like Joselito, winning both ears
In a country field in Roscommon, for the sake of some
                                        daffodils.

What happened in fact is this. I drove on
Without stopping, but remembering that old bull
And the desolate green spears furled downwards all round
                                        his feet
In a field where there had once been golden trumpets.

At the Grave of William Joyce

Those who are scarcely old enough, as I am not,
To remember his broadcasts, but know the name,
May accept the title of this poem with misgivings.

Why remember the great traitor? Lord Haw-Haw
Betrayed his country to speak out for the Nazis.
What more is there to say?

He betrayed nothing. William Joyce
Was an Irish citizen who defended his country
Against the common enemy, as he saw her,
With the weapon of words. I remember him here,

A resident now of the Galway he was born in,
And wanted to come back to, and has done so.

Let him lie easier in his native soil
Than ever he did on the treacherous pillow of
                                        propaganda.

Remember, poets.
There is only one treason, the treason to language.

The Girls of Kylemore Abbey

Imagine a lyric
Sung to a mountain tune along the shore of a lake
In Connemara, stone upon stone upon stone upon stone.

Five girls in water.

The first girl, whose face we do not see,
Is wearing a bathing-dress
Ruched below the knees, the starched Victorian cotton
Sopping wet over her ample breasts.

The second girl, your grandmother,
Waves for the cameras. She is wearing
A one-piece swimming-costume
In some clinging woollen material. Her nipples
Protrude in the cold.

The third girl, in a 1950s bikini
Of some itsi-bitsi lurex,
Pouts with her hand on her hip, all Jane Russell
And promising bulges. This is your mother.

The fourth girl
Is topless. Her magnificent, free
Bosom lifts from a rock, in pale splendour. But her sex
Glows through transparent knickers. This is you.

Daughter, daughter, you say,
Calling to the fifth girl, who is only nine,
Why do you go naked? The lake
Is full of wanton men, from many centuries,

And all are watching.

The Child Husband

In those days, we had a little room of the house
Nicknamed the seraglio, fifteen feet by nine
With a white dado irrationally, three doors
And a sort of linen cupboard at one end.

My pretty wife would lie on the couch, for hours,
Looking at nothing, since there were no windows,
Or reading from *The Arabian Nights*, for fun,
Or simply falling asleep, with her crocodile.

It was a strange life. Coffee at ten
From a beaten brassware pot, with Turkish delight
And then a glass of port, or Courvoisier.
No one noticed how slow the time went.

The odalisques on the wall reclined, and smiled,
The covers fell from the stools onto the spiders,
And no one cared. Outside a prodigal sun
Gilded the moulting lilies. It was September

In a kind of Ireland no one remembers now,
A careless, distant Ireland where there were prayers
Every Sunday for the fallen in the Boer War
And the travelling children ate our bread in the road.

If there was a fantasy in creating a harem
Out of a few old cushions, and a plushy toy,
Mixing the colours right, and providing incense
Out of a jar from the bathroom, Lifebuoy soap

And essence of cloves, wanting a copper gong
To be brought from the stables, and lacking charm
To persuade James into bringing one, who cares,
Who ever cared, and who will come to upbraid us?

A Ruined Castle

Crouching, as I crouch now,
I flounder crab-wise across tussocks
Towards the keep, and what remains.

The biggest ivy-tree I've ever seen
Knots in a corner of a tower. Inside,
The usual sheep-droppings,
A barrel vault, and a window.

The steps are deep, hard-climbing. Imagine
Tumbling that steepness, wielding a cutlass!

Then, upstairs,
On what is now a twenty-one foot square terrace
With a view of the Ballyhoura Hills,
An embrasure, and two stone seats.

He must have sat there
With Sir Guyon, or Belphoebe,
Watching the rain, remembering Cheapside.

I hear the baby crying,
The sound of the burning straw falling,
See them run:

Peregrine, Sylvanus, Elizabeth

And Edmund Spenser, leaving the last book
Of *The Faerie Queene*, in the flames.

Elegy for the Grey Kitten

Three days later, hearing of his death,
It still brings tears to my eyes
Collecting pussy willow, or drinking martini
On the terrace, without him. He would have lain
Washing his beautiful grey fur, in that sunbeam.
Now he lies under a flat stone, by the gate
Where James put him, on Friday evening, in the twilight.

I walk by, scarcely pausing. But I remember
His one green eye, and his great weight before
That final thinness, the little lump on his back
The vet said must have been a sebaceous cyst.

It doesn't matter. Cancer will kill a cat.
He knew he was going. Went out, after a meal
And lay in the dark, under a concrete post
In the wood, hearing the crows building their nests
For the last time. There James found him dead.

I was away, in Holland. He must have known,
I tell myself, and been happy, knowing.
I wouldn't see him weak and tired at the end
But only remember his quick flight up a tree,
The hard spring of his fur, and the purr he learned
Lying hour after hour, pleased in my lap.

He was a good cat, whatever that means.

A Celebration

Fires had been kindled on the twenty-third
Along the bog road from the hospital.
People had lit them for the solstice. Now
They seemed a celebration of our child
Who had just been born. It was the Feast of
The Sacred Heart. Midsummer madness, too,
And everything was cured, and had come through.

I drove past, smiling, watching the flames rise
And the sparks settle, and the children run.
I saw this once in Finland, years before,
Only in Finland, never in England,
The same bright, atavistic urge for summer
To burn away in one convulsive blaze
And leave no cinder. This was just the same.

I thought about our child. Her sudden head
Through your strained flesh, and then the slippery limbs,
The twisting marble of the cord, the tripes
And purplish ox-heart she had fattened on
Through nine months of your dreaming heaviness.
Now you were smaller, and our girl was born,
Red as the sun, to celebratory fires.

I drove on to my future. Fatherhood
Like vernix now lay white around my brow,
A caul of love, a laurel wreath of joy.
The years declining offered me their arms
Like glowing embers, and I warmed my age
In growing hope. Here was the fiery heir,
A queen of Ireland in her vitreous cot.

I felt my leg revive. Stepped out at home
Into a morning new as light at Moyne,
Sniffing the air. Here was another day
Wherein you waking would arouse and feed
Her sleeping lips, toy with her pixy ears
And know the mystery of genesis
First hand. Happy, I went indoors to sleep.

Upon the Lady in the Oval Frame

Life is a matter of inventing stories.

Your great-aunt Agatha, for example,
The lace and gingham one
In the hall.

Do you remember the times
When you went to tea with her, pushing crumbs
Through the holes in her fretwork chair?
You were five, rising six, a serious, miniature blonde.

I see her naughty
As you were, in the heady sixties,
Giggling and skipping amongst her grandmother's
                                        knick-knacks

With a jar of itching powder. What a woman!
She ends up, I suppose,
On the railings outside Buckingham Palace,
A reluctant suffragette.

After the jail sentence, a long retirement, perhaps
In Cheadle Hulme. (This is a very British picture.)

Then the Bournvita, nights
Listening to Lord Haw-Haw on the wireless
And a death by asphyxiation, leaving the gas on.

Nothing too Betjeman, you see.
Simply a traditional English life
Lived out in a gilt frame, with ice-blue eyes
And no conscience. Agatha, of course, is the Greek for
good.

So knock your nail in, and let her hang
Between the stag's head, and the print of Cromwell,
Your family gauleiter.

Of course, she was no relation.
In actual fact, I bought the bitch in Cromer.

But the blue eyes, the blue eyes make me wonder.

An Incident from
the Nineteenth Century

'I am Count von Puckler-Muskau,
May I see your lovely house?'

'I don't know. I'll ask the mistress.
Sit and browse here, Puckler-Muskau.'

Through the window, on the ladies,
Fell a sickly Irish sun.

Count von Puckler-Muskau's toothpick
Flickered in his open jaws.

Upstairs, the mistress in her knickers
Plucked her eyebrows for a ball.

She thought about the German tourist
Freezing in the servants' hall.

'Bring him up, dear. There's a darling.
Is he handsome? Puckler-Muskau?

Hmnn, it rings a distant bell.'
Naked in her knickers, bobbing

Barefoot on the marble stairs –
von Puckler-Muskau nearly vanished.

This was better than Leap Castle
Where he'd slept with seven virgins.

'Good morning, Count von Puckler-Muskau.
Take me now, or take me never.

Charles is hunting. He'll be back soon.
You have half an hour precisely.'

So they did it in the gun-room –
Smell of oil and Purdey's rifles.

Trifling with his penis later
The mistress yawned and kissed his forehead.

'Charles is back. You'd better go now.
I hear the roan mare in the yard.'

'Who was that?' Charles asked at luncheon,
Nodding at the passing carriage.

'Oh, some German tourist, darling.
He never left his name or card.'

A Cheer for the Baronet's Widow

Somewhere in Wexford, the novelist, Molly Keane,
Writes about great houses, the way they have always been,

Drawing largely on her own digested experience
Of what it was like to mount a gelding, or mend a fence.

You could say, it's a waste of time, outdated stuff,
The world of 1989 in Ireland has problems enough

Of its own, unemployment, violence in the north,
And so on, and so forth.

But it isn't entirely inappropriate
To delineate the exact, forgotten cut

Of a huntsman's jacket, or a lady's ball gown,
Or even some scandalous goings-on in Mitchelstown

In 1930. Years leave their own silt of mood
And how the evils of primogeniture have accrued

May still be a fit subject for these parlous times,
And the bishops' anxieties, and the partisan crimes.

The Biography
of Bananas

Not everyone would know
From the colour of his skin
And his broad, human face
That he was born at sea
In the bottom of a boat.

Some say so. And some say
That he was born on land
In a Republic of
Central America
In a city on a hill.

At any rate, the sun
Burnishing, as it does,
All brilliant, furry things
Has tanned him to a hue
The exact shade of a calf.

Me Tarzan, and you Jane.
Well, anyway, the times
Allow no monkeying
About with how things start.
Bananas burst full grown

Into a Worcester shop
And here he is, and smiles,
Much older than he was
And even nicer, too,
A quite essential ape.

A Poet on the Tiles

He had never before he was sixty, picked up a prostitute
Or written a hexameter. The combination was likely to
                                         prove fruitful,
He reflected, eyeing the smoking girl in the Earl's Court
                                         Road.

Jackass was actually sixty-seven, the girl twenty,
As he later discovered. 'It's a cold night,' he began, 'would
                                         you like
Some coffee, or just a chat first?' The girl eyed him,
Speculating, no doubt, about his virility, his cash,
And whether he was a nutter. Deciding yes, he supposed,
                                         she shook
Her rather greasy black curls, and refused his coffee.

But he saw the glint in her eyes, as he fondled his
                                         bulging wallet.
'Well, how about a walk, then?' 'Up to my room?' This
                                         was quicker
Than he had expected, but quite in order. He nodded,
                                         breathing,
It must be stressed, rather hard as he climbed the
                                         numerous stairs.
I draw a veil over the bed, as she did not. The pink
                                         curtains,
The plastic chandelier and the bedside photos – forget
                                         them.

Jackass performed quite well. She yawned afterwards,
                                         lighting
A gauloise. It was all rather nouvelle vague, salacious but
                                         tasteful,
And fifty quid seemed a perfectly decent swindle,
                                         considering.

Back in the two o'clock road, he squared his
                              cashmere shoulders
And strode like John Wayne to the Wimpey Bar. It was
                                        closed.

And closed were the lips of Reason, accusing, the voice of
                                        Aids
Murmuring warnings. He fondled the prick in his pocket.
                              And not all
The angels in Heaven could stop him feeling a sense of
                              well-being.
Homeric verses. The beat of oars. The oiled breasts
Of Nausicaa and her maidens, lifting easily in the
                              moonlight.

The wily Odysseus rowed to his bed-sit, dreaming of next
                                        time
And the squirming bellies groaned for ease in the brine.
                              And all this
Might have happened exactly thus, but it didn't, walking
                              home
After a chaste late supper with Helen, not having laid her,
And after reading *Amours de Voyage* on the train to
                              Bedford.

And if these be not hexameters, tell me. Were Arthur
                              Hugh Clough's?
And if this be no vision of glory, tell me. What sort of
                              dream is?

The Sister Islands

Those were the sister islands,
Two jewels in the sea,
Emeralds on water,
But neither was for me.

They made a foreign marriage
Far away from home,
They paced with veils and chanting
And took the vows for Rome.

But later there came trouble
And Henry was its name.
One sister proved a harlot
And one became a dame.

I married America,
I got well away.
But I dream of the island sisters
Every day.

Emeralds on water,
Green like the sea,
Both meant trouble
But neither was for me.

The Postman

Past a green hole in the wall
With VR on it,
He drives his orange van.

'In the 1920s
You wore a bottle round your neck,
If you couldn't speak English.'

Is that so? Thus Matt,
The Republican postman
Who brings me letters from England,

Smiles through dark glasses,
His peaked cap
A reminder of military glory.

Nothing smiles
More easily than victory
On the former landlords

Who still wash their Jaguars
Before the portals
Of an Irish excellence.

But who cares? Not me
Nor the educated postman
Who remembers Patrick Pearsse

And can recite his poems
In a language
Neither Yeats nor Wilde could speak.

The Stepfather

Sometimes, because it must be easier, I suppose,
I remember the intent young policemen with their pencils
And the troubled, weary girl, going over it all again,

Months later. And sometimes, I try to be rather braver
Or more worried, and see the scene in the rented flat,
The dark hall, the sunlight, and the little boy running
                                                    away

When the man said, 'If you don't do what I tell you,
I'll kill your brother.' But it isn't easy, and I shift
Away to a beach, and the girl in a tight rose
                                bathing-costume,

And the willowy boys going by in their bulging trunks.
It isn't easy, even for me. Remembering nights
Brushing her nipples by accident

In the bear-hug of a fatherly embrace. Think of him,
Yes, whoever it was, watching her day after day perhaps,
In that hot sun, on that burning intolerable patio

In the middle of nowhere, cowed, ignored and bored
And able, if he only took a chance, to do what he wanted
And achieve uniqueness. 'He asked me if it was the first
                                                    time

And I said it was. He said I would always remember him
Because it was the first time.' The cunt, the fucker,
All the dirty words come up like vomit, and curdle

In the mouth of judgement. And meanwhile, the man is
                                                    still
At large in his conscience, out on the street in his jeans
With his dark face and his mole, that she remembers,

And the questions are going on, are still going on.

Lady M

Somewhere in an attic room
There's a print of Lady M,
Features accurate as doom
Cut like facets of a gem.
She was younger then than now
But no more arcane and fine.
Let grapes wither on the bough,
They mature as noble wine.

Drink your rum and coke like blood,
Lift your glass and toast her wealth,
Spilled and risen from the mud
Mounted on intemperate health.
Let bright anger tip her blade
With no time to suffer fools,
Wantoning will all that's made
Subject to unpassioned rules.

Lady M was bright and fair,
Lady M was dark and still,
She could ride a horse to death,
She could break an eagle's will.
Sound the horn and call the hounds,
Lady M will ride today
Over fifty miles of grounds
Frosted by the fogs of May.

Lady M, I like your looks
And your tall Palladian hall
And your miles of wandering brooks
Where the bright kingfishers fall.
Stables hold your straw and dung
But no hunters leap and neigh
Nor strong dogs group and give tongue.
The violent hunt is long away.

Age must come and smite the best
Answering the call of skin
Weaving for its winter vest
February, and the whinn.
Cry for beauty, and delight,
Savour what is left to come,
Praise that taut and yellowish white
Stretched like parchment on a drum.

Sarah

He was married to another, she was only that one's friend,
But she persevered, her friend died. She took over in the
                                                        end.

Taught the children, brought them up well, helped her
                                    husband with his boats,
Oversaw the chicken farm, and showed the strangers to
                                                their coats.

Plenty of them came to dinner, some to breakfast and for
                                                        tea,
But few were so persistent as the four men from the
                                                ministry.

The words they spoke were plain and brutal, but they
                                    made it sound polite.
'The country needs more sanitoria, your house is on a
                                            perfect site.'

So her husband took their money. 'After all, he had no
                                                choice.'
I see her say it from her armchair, with a tremble in her
                                                voice.

I see her in her wooden cottage, pouring tea and serving
                                                cake,
Remembering the deep betrayal the sale they forced would
                                                shortly make:

The demolition gang, the masons breaking down what
                                        might have stood
Still, into future generations, above the water, in its wood.

'Nothing now remains, no trace of that great mansion, his
                                                and mine.'
Only the trees remain, and Sarah burning with rage at
                                                eighty-nine.

You can rise above your station, you can hunt with horse
                                                and hound,
But they'll take what you inherit, and they'll smash it to
                                                the ground.

A Fine Day for Killing
a Constable

Says he, I'm sorry,
But this bus has just been hijacked by the I.R.A.

Breakfast will be served at Shannon,
Settle back and enjoy yourselves.

No, madam, toilet facilities -
Of a temporary nature, I'm afraid -
Will not be available before Ballinasloe.

There are chess sets in the back of the seats
In front of you. The music you can hear playing
Is Fingal's Cave, by Felix Mendelssohn-
Bartholdy, I believe.

Going well, so far.
But where next?

Something about the old days, perhaps,
When it was all still
Night-sticks on the foreskin. But it's

Different nowadays, eh Jock? eh, laddie?

Not so much of the fucking Micks now, eh?
Show a little more politeness, don't we?

Hold his balls, Seamus,
While I juggle with them.

Yes, it's a fine day for killing a constable.

The Birth of a Star

Ludovic Caesar Bunratty Bingham
Knew all the songs, and he could sing 'em.

Twanging his little electric guitar
He dreamed of one day becoming a star.

He went down to the pub with a rebel air
And his ukulele in good repair.

And there he met, on an office outing,
Virginia Chetwode Follicle-Flouting,

Who smiled at him. And, in holy wedlock,
Persuaded the boy to erase each dreadlock

And, wearing a suit, which made him look foetal,
Come on like an early emergent Beatle.

Not George or Paul or John, but Ringo,
The pizazz of a black, and the gall of a gringo.

Well, to cut a long story short, he grew famous
And changed his name to O'Fortescue Seamus

And now he sings nightclub Irish ditties
To millionaire Kits and their perfumed kitties.

It could happen to you, and to U 2, too –
A night on the tiles, then a life in Who's Who.

The Impossible Guest

Imagine the impossible guest:
His hair is greasy, he speaks mainly Spanish,
He behaves like a Nazi.

So far, so bad. Add in that he smokes,
Including during meals, a foul pipe,
Apologising, and asking if you would get him an ash-
                                          tray.

His cases, which you have carried from the station
On the hottest day of the year, O.K.
So that wasn't his fault, but it doesn't help,
Are tartan rexine, and stuffed with pornography.

His telephone calls, after midnight,
On your phone, to his wife,
Are long, loud, and recriminatory.

Your grasp of Spanish is just enough
To pick up, ear ground to the key-hole,
That he isn't arranging the date of his flight home.

Most of the time he seems, and is,
Drunk, on your Guinness. He breathes crumbs
Over the Norfolk jacket you have bought him
Out of a sense of guilt for the olden days.

After all, he was something else then,
A hell of a lad, as you were,
A real shit-raiser.

Then, wham.

He mentions, quite casually,
During a candlelit dinner, that he has multiple
                                    sclerosis.

Red faces all round, yes?

But you still pay the two hundred and forty-
                                         nine
Irish quid, and ship him back
Fast, to his pad in the west. It seems best.

I mean, for Christ's sake,
What else can you do
With a snoring farter
Who ogles your friend's wife?

Damned if I know.

The degenerative process advances fast.

The Betjeman of
the Irish Bungalow

I crouch on celadon moquette
And hum through lanes the Gardai vet
In search of some one-storey pet.

Wheeling my avocado Ford
I never never once grow bored
Emptying out my treasure-hoard.

I haul them in from near and far
Where coach-lamps glimmer by a car,
Roncalli close to Shangri-la.

The greyhounds lounge along a wall,
A sunburst fronts the entrance hall
Where Maeve and Kevin bounce a ball.

The palmtrees in their urns lie curled,
Acanthus leaves are nicely furled.
A priestly languor rules the world.

Religion means you keep things nice.
You can afford them, at the price.
A grant from Dublin pays a slice.

Now westering, questioning sinks the sun
As I drive past admiring one
Whose balustrade has just begun.

The Twilight of
the Ascendancy

Good afternoon. So good
Of you to have come. Here we all are.

This is Fiona, my grand-daughter, she's
Making a box
For her douroucouli.

This is Alaric, my grand-father, he's
Cleaning his pipe
Into a jam-jar. He's rather deaf, I'm afraid.
AREN'T YOU, OLD FELLOW?

This is Edwina, my wife's
Lady's maid, she's
Percolating coffee, in a colander. Will you
Have some?

This is Hengist, my
Faithful hound, actually
He's a bit of a mongrel, a bit manky.

And what's he doing? I think he must be
Spring-cleaning his equipment.

Who is this, darling? Ah yes, this
Is Roger Longrod, who
Does the drains. Thank you, Roger,

There's no need to shake hands.

And this is Pipistrelle, the
Baby-sitter, she
Rocks Fiona to sleep every night
With her krumhorn.

This is the drawing-room, and this
Is the room
For folding newspapers. Mind the drip,

That's Edgar, paring his nails. A cousin, yes.

Anyway, there you have it. Lorimer Hall
In all its glory. I look
Forward to your book, especially the photographs
Of the dove-cotes and the footmen's loo.

Mind the caravan, as you leave,
In the drive. We have a visit
From Oonagh, my mother-in-law.

And this is her family, yes. They deal
In scrap metal. All fourteen of them.

Sorry about the mess
And your exhaust. But they're easily replaceable,
Aren't they?

Do come again, when you've time
And the energy. We'll do the cow-byres, too.

Crow Shoot

Over eight hundred crows fell
In forty minutes. Four of the guns
Handed their double-barrelled Purdeys to Mason, three to
                                                    Driver.

The bodies were piled in the forecourt, behind the urns
And the statue of Artemis. They made a heap in the
                                        smoky sun
Like the Aztec pyramids of skulls at Tenochtitlan
Or the body-count of Genghiz Khan after Bokhara.

This was a dream, you say. Perhaps. But walk
Over the cobbles near to the well and the sewer-pipes
And your boots will strike bones. I know. I do
This every morning on my way to empty the dish-water
And muck out the pigs, and I remember the crow-shoots.

I wake in the night, hearing the startled cries
Of those boys in the flues, black as your hat,
Some of them, from Jamaica, born in Shoreditch
To their smothering trade, apprenticed
At seven years old.

Outside my window, a rook beats at the panes.

The turf fire blazes now
In the grate of the smoking-room, and the men tell
Old stories of blood and ire, how someone fell
At the flooded brook, and someone face down
In the dung-pile, and all was well, it was a fine day
For hunting, yes, or sweeping chimneys, in Anglo-Ireland.

No, sir. I was born in the north, parents from Cardiff.
But you learn the score. You start to feel how they feel.

Crows, you know, and Aztecs. Climbing-boys and the Irish.

A Conversation with Grandfather

And where were you the night
We burned Mount Sion? Were
You in the passing crowd, or safe
At home in Ballyruin?

That's me in the cloth cap, Declan,
Your old father's father, seventy years
Back, near as damn it. I was
Up there by the colonnades.

                I remember,
I remember, all those beer-flushed faces,
James and Paddy, Rush and Edwards, all
Ploughed under like the landlords.

                Who
Was there, was Jimmy Daly, Jimmy from the forge? Was
He there?

                I don't know, lad. I
Remember curtains blazing, plaster breaking, taken
All in all, it was a fine night, better
Than a football riot.

                Meanwhile, far away in London,
Lord and Lady Simper-Footwell, stuffed their hearts
With spit and mustard, largely ignorant
Of what was happening, idle at some Chelsea Ball.

Good riddance to them. Yes, I'm sorry
For those bricks and mortar, crashing joists
And ancient floorboards. Houses don't have feelings,
Do they? Lucky for us that they don't.

Ruining two centuries' handwork, Irish masons
Laid the stones. Irish work and Irish genius
Pissed on for a night of spite.

Still, it happened. It's forgotten,
It's remembered. Well, who cares?

Lord and Lady Simper-Footwell and the men
Who burned their mansion, all

Except your poor old Grandad,
Roast in hell, or roost in heaven. Give

Or take another five years, you can
Spread manure on
What's left. Fallen arches, twisted ivy,
Holes in walls that stood for pride.

Have another Guinness, Declan. I'd not
Rack your pretty head with bothering
About an old war. That, or any other. Drink, and smile.

Upon Maud Gonne

She must have been a big girl
  To flatten that long couch-grass
And it wet and springy after the rain, too.

Imagine her sun-bathing nude
  With her ears back and her legs bent
In the field. And then the visitors coming tramping

Waving their poetry books and their trunks
  And braying out their praise of the ruin.
It must have been a nasty shock for the girl.

Anyway, she ran hell for leather
  To the bullocks, heading through those brambles
Fringing the stable-block, and she was gone.

Make a note, Willie, one of the visitors
  Said, in the back of your Blake now.
She would give you a fine simile for the mountain hare.

A Catholic Childhood

Half-way along the muddy tunnel,
We turned back, slightly disconcerted, and worried.
There seemed to have been a coffin below the mud
When Catherine went in over her ankles.
A plank, anyway. Something under the slime.
We thought it had been a route to a family vault
From the sense of a body underneath her wellingtons.
Or was it a priest's escape? Some of us thought that,
Since there was room for a broad-shouldered man
Lifting a sconce, lighting his way with a candle.
Then someone pointed to a cleft, where water flowed,
A soakaway for some kind of sluice, or sewer.
Waste products were the least glamorous option,
If the most likely. Nothing seemed worse
Than sinking deeper into ancient ordure.
Grave-mould or candle-grease, we could accept.
So we turned back, fouled by whatever it was,
Not having reached, or seen, our goal. Whether corpses,
Treasure, or stagnant pools waited, who could say?
Back at the dozing house, there was tea in the sun,
Cucumber sandwiches, plum cake and buns,
And we ate well. But what I most remember
Is the dark, unearthly precipitate on our soles
And how hard it was to get off, even with knives.

Even with masses later, even with prayers.

Browning in the South

Yes, he used to come here with his wife, painting
Those Arab oils: camels, and tents, and sand,
You know the sort. There's one on your bedroom wall
Where he's made Bantry Bay into a desert
With a girl carrying a water-pot on her head
Like a red tulip. The pot may even have *been*
A tulip, from behind the maze. There are still some
　　　　　　　　　　　　　　　　　growing there.
Painters are funny people. He would often get up
Before dawn, and do a hand-stand
In the grass, in the dew. It made me cough in my tea
With astonishment, bending to light the gas-stove
With my husband still unshaved. As for his wife,
Well, she was the usual artist's help-meet,
Blonde and mousey, bit of an indrawn type
I ought to say, except in bed, no doubt.
But I never saw that. Heard it, though?
Come now, Mr Browning, you wouldn't expect
The inside story of a great Irish painter
Complete with his love life for a half hour's
Benevolent, easy chat in the bushes, now would you?
It's back to my sinks and ovens for me, and for you
A brisk turn round the several shrubberies before dinner
And a fine sea-trout, and a bottle of hock, and a night
Alone in your room with that elongated oil
And the mystery of it, left untouched by enquiry.
Don't spoil it all with a tart, salacious story
Extorted for a few pounds from a willing servant.
Let the wall own its truth. Watch it, and muse.

Balzac

After midnight, he would come into the room
And light a candle, and take his stand
At the sloping desk, and begin to write.

Outside, it was raining hard. You could hear the wind
Sometimes, covering the wood
Like the wing of a hawk. You could smell the mould rising.

Those were intractable years. The world
Went on and on about its own business, watching
No one writing late at night in a lonely room

Miles above Paris. Not even Honoré de Balzac,
Whose real name was Balsa. Yes, like the wood
You used to carve horses from.

Imagine carving a novelist,
Someone no bigger than your own hand at first,
From the whole career of Balzac, statue by Rodin and all.

It would take a long knife. A lifetime's effort
Against the grain of the language, spinning yarns
Into a cardigan of laughter. Try it and see.

I know, George. I tried it myself once
Before I gave up the world for poetry
And died running guns. Go back to Ireland

And study your own people, forget Lady Cunard.
Remember Balzac dying at fifty
Three months after a late marriage, worn out by Russia.

Nothing matters except the olive volumes,
Gilt on their spines, treading the shelf to infinity.
Keep going. Up on tiptoe, until your ankles ache.

There's my boy. You'll be a novelist yet.

A Poem for a Martian

Sometimes the glasses were like wine-glasses,
Like chimneys, like anti-aircraft guns,
Like girls' nipples reaching forward to be stroked.

The weight of cold iron, the sense of a car
Straining forward to some unknown destination
Through a night of rain and blood. Romantic viewings!

But then the glasses would have to have been on a table
Turned by 1930s hands, or by dumb waiters,
And the chimneys would have to have been on New York
                                                    skylines

Where the girls were stacked, 1940s girls
With headlamps you could see to drive by
Even in fog, even with the enemy airplanes

Coming in low, out of the rain and flack,
And our lives focussing on them, like wartime binoculars.

The Ballad of
Gabriele D'Annunzio

a burlesque

I

Gabriele D'Annunzio wrote much verse
Which was rarely decent, and never terse.

He specialized in a sort of novel
Which made well-brought-up young women grovel.

The ladies all said that he was cruel
And he lost his hair one day in a duel.

A doctor, to make the bastard placid,
Doused his wounds with a bottle of acid.

One day he met the Duse, his Muse,
And seduced her on a Mediterranean cruise.

Poems came slowly from his pen
But he oozed them down like an antique hen.

There were classic tales with a modern twist
Every time Eleonora was kissed.

II

But he ditched the Duse for a marchioness
Who straddled her pony without a dress.

This cropful beauty, whose breasts could stun,
Got cancer, survived, and became a nun.

She died in an avalanche in a storm
Trying to keep her conscience warm.

Gabriele grieved, but his poems got better
When they were conceived in a French letter.

He had so many debts, when he sold his horses
Suicide or emigration were his only courses.

He chose the second, he packed his bags,
He shed no tears for those Florentine shags,

There were more to come. Things were getting madder.
Life seemed an ever-expanding ladder.

III

He emigrated. Destination, France,
A suave Don Quixote with a trouser-sheathed lance,

His Sancho Panza, a world-weary count
With a jewelled tortoise he could no longer mount.

For six sharp months on a mounting spiral
Gabriele's diseases were largely viral.

The cocottes filed through his bedroom fast,
They could hardly wait for his lines to be cast.

So the months rolled by in blood and curses
With reams of women, and sheaves of verses.

Gabriele was the flavour of the year in Paris,
He even exceeded the lewd Frank Harris.

But at last he retired to a house plein-air
With a Lesbian, American millionaire.

IV

Down here by the sea he could rest and be painted
While a Junoesque Russian countess fainted.

Oral homage was paid, while she lay in her void,
In the manner her Italian lover enjoyed.

The serious business was a raunchy ballet,
The rumour of Cannes, and the rage of Calais.

The star was a slimline Jewish lady
Who might once have danced for Diamond Jim Brady.

But now a-quiver, on a rocky bastion,
She stripped her bosom as St Sebastian.

The count adored her, the painter sketched,
And her dart-fine body was nightly stretched.

Well, Gabriele, courting her with his cornetto,
Required inspiration for the libretto.

V

Meanwhile, the world-soul, growing weary
Began to find the arts of peace too dreary.

Europe went to war. Gabriele, in order
To become patriotic, re-crossed the border.

From every balcony on Italian soil
He urged his countrymen to rise and toil.

So that Lombardy, normally the land of light,
Was consumed by a rather surprising need to fight.

The voice of this midget with the awful breath
Drove cowards to ignore their fear of death.

Gabriele enlisted. He was fifty-two,
As frail as his friend, the Count Montesquieu.

But he marched with the infantry, he ran up hills,
He was in at all the most important kills.

VI

He lodged in Venice, in the grandest style,
He groped for victory up every aisle.

He bombed Vienna, not with bombs but paper,
It was quite an unprecedented caper.

In an Austrian harbour, he leaned from a boat
And left an insulting message afloat.

Oh, it was fun. He loved that war,
When he was wounded, he came back for more.

One day he crash-landed. They thought he would die.
He lay in darkness, he lost an eye.

Death was for real. So was blindness.
The world was ruled by loving-kindness.

And his pretty daughter, while he eased his phallus,
Looked after him in a smouldering palace

VII

On the Grand Canal. Things were much the same
With the gondoliers and the birds on the game.

This was the hour of a mignon in gauze
And an aigrette bobbing without a pause,

And a startling memoir, in astonishing prose,
Which, for once, got up nobody's nose.

The poseur had done it. He stole the fleece,
He churned out a bloody masterpiece.

Why, even the choosy Ernest Hemingway
Agreed it was lovely, at the end of the day.

When the war was over, Gabriele was tired.
Life seemed a little bit underfired.

The Fiume Question soon brought an answer.
He would scrap his planes and his pestering dancer.

VIII

He would leave and annexe a Hungarian port,
He'd be a prince, the Renaissance sort.

So he marched by night with a hundred men;
Well, he drove in his Fiat to Fiume, and then –

Why, the garrison surrendered! They unlatched the gate
And a full general received Gabriele in state.

He was elected governor, philosopher-king.
He could do just about anything.

He pirated ships, he defied Giolitti,
Gabriele was regent of the holocaust city.

He made laws and speeches, he made love and war.
What else is absolute power for?

People sailed from far and wide for the screwing.
But its very licence was the place's undoing.

IX

The Italian government bided its time
And at Christmas it struck, like a claw from the slime.

A battleship bombarded the town
And brought the dream of D'Annunzio down.

With a bandage of blood streaming round his head
Gabriele was taken from his mansion for dead.

He revived, though, hearing the words, thou sinner,
And dismissed his confessor for a slap-up dinner.

At the rear of his column of legionnaires
He went home to his rhymes and his bed-bound mares.

Well, we hear no more now for several years.
All was sure to end, you will say, in tears.

But it didn't. This early-retiring Attila
Bought himself a dilapidated Lake Garda villa.

X

This had once belonged to Richard Wagner's wife.
He bought it for the nation, with a lease for life.

That brought in money like a barrel of grain
And Gabriele was never short of cash again.

He encrusted the front of his villa with Latin,
He slept in a coffin which he lined with satin.

He built a live theatre where he read
With his Viennese aeroplane slung overhead.

And, best of all, to let fantasy rip
In his garden he planted half a battleship.

One day on the deck, a quartet of strings
Grated while Mussolini said several things.

He'd ridden from Rome, flanked by motor-bikes,
And he emphasized both his likes and dislikes.

XI

He would happily initiate, and this was his mission,
Of D'Annunzio's works, a collected edition.

But he didn't want Gabriele, in a blaze of luce,
Getting any big ideas of replacing the Duce.

Well, what of the women? Why, some of them died.
Eleonora, ungratified.

Gabriele drove to her last rites in Rome,
A wizened figure in monochrome.

But at home he blossomed. He tried out boys,
He was full of the waning, senile joys.

At length, after creeping to seventy-five,
He grew bored of being so long alive.

He wrote one last time to his mistress to court her
And fell dead, asking for a glass of water.

XII

Gabriele D'Annunzio, this is your life.
You lived on the brink of perpetual strife,

You had no morals, you were bald and randy
And the fascists found that you came in handy.

Your funeral brought out the blackshirts and girls
And your wife by Mussolini in her hennaed curls.

You never divorced her, you stood by the church,
You left a dozen good friends in the lurch,

You furnished your house, you wrote fine books,
You got your picture painted by Romaine Brooks.

That was something. There you are,
The earliest twentieth-century star,

The original operatic hero
With a current popularity rating of zero.

XIII

If only you'd worked on a score for Puccini
Or had this ballad written by Seamus Heaney!

Hail and farewell, in the name of farce
Under the sign of the upturned arse,

May your best work survive as a pregnant motto
Byronically carved in some lecherous grotto

There to be read, for a fanciful spoof,
By a couple engaged in soixante-neuf

Like the loving pair on your favourite ring
Said to have been forged at Mayerling.

Enough, D'Annunzio, hail and farewell
And now, like Don Juan, away to Hell

To burn with the best in a blaze of glory
And only survive as a cautionary story.

XIV

Supposing that you were a feminist
With a knight in your bed and a hawk on your fist,

A fifteenth-century sort of girl
With a sword in your sheath and your hair in a twirl,

Or even the twentieth-century sort
With a job at Virago and a friend at Earl's Court,

Would you offer this poem to someone dear
As a dreadful example of what to fear?

Are these the attitudes of modern Man?
Well, at least a few of the stanzas scan.

There may even, under the lines, be a moral
Bright as a jewel, and as tough as coral.

Did Gabriele die of despair?
Or was it only that foetid air?